John Goodman

The Golden Rule

The Royal Law of Equity

John Goodman

The Golden Rule
The Royal Law of Equity

ISBN/EAN: 9783742831200

Manufactured in Europe, USA, Canada, Australia, Japa

Cover: Foto ©Andreas Hilbeck / pixelio.de

Manufactured and distributed by brebook publishing software
(www.brebook.com)

John Goodman

The Golden Rule

THE
Golden Rule,

Or, THE
ROYAL LAW
OF
EQUITY
EXPLAINED.

Ὁι ἄνθρωποι οἴκοθεν γινώσκομὲν τὸ δέον.
Theophyl. in Rom.

LONDON,

Printed by *Samuel Roycroft*, for *Robert Clavell* at the *Peacock* at the West-End of St. *Pauls*, 1688.

THE

Golden Rule,

Or, THE

ROYAL LAW

OF

EQUITY

EXPLAINED.

THERE never was any Law, Human or Divine; nor any Principle of Common Reason and Philosophy , which hath been more univerſally Received and Acknowledged , than that Aphoriſm

of

of our Saviours, which he delivers *Matt.7.12. Whatsoever ye would that Men should do unto you, do ye even so unto them.* It hath been Admir'd both by Jews and Gentils, as well as Christians: Amongst the former, it was the Cognizance of the greatest and most eminent Sect or Party of them, *viz.* the School of *Hillel.* Amongst the latter, It is well known that *Severus* (one of the Best and Wisest of the Roman Emperours) was so taken with it, that He not only had this Saying frequently in his Mouth, but caused it to be Inscribed as his Motto upon his Banners. In a word, It is a Maxim subscribed to and owned by the Men of all Ages, Countries, Sects, Qualities, and Conditions; for indeed (as we shall see Anon) the Reason of it is as clear as the Light, the Date of it is as Ancient as Mankind, and its Obligation as Indissoluble as the very Frame of Nature.

Besides

Besides all this, It is evident at
the firſt Bluſh, that there neither is,
nor ever was, any Precept of any
Religion or Inſtitution whatſoever,
which was or could be more exactly
Calculated for the Improving of the
State of Mankind, or for the Main-
taining of Juſtice and Equity,
Peace and Love in the World, than
this is.

It may juſtly ſeem a Wonder
therefore how it ſhould come to
paſs, that ſo little Fruit ſhould
grow from ſo pregnant a Root!
And that when all Men ſo unani-
mouſly pretend to ſuch a common
Principle of Equity, there ſhould
notwithſtanding be ſo much Un-
eaſineſs, and ſo many Complaints
in the World; ſuch Frauds and
Injuſtice, Oppreſſions and Perſecu-
tions; and ſuch mutual Accuſations
and Recriminations. And to Aſſoil
this Difficulty, one muſt of neceſſity
either paſs a very ſevere Cenſure

A 4   upon

upon a great part of Mankind, as acting inconfiftently with themfelves, and contradicting their Avowed Principles by their Practices; or elfe on the other fide, one muft fuppofe that as great a Party of Men as the former, do not underftand this Common Rule, or have not confidered the Force and Obligation of it

Now the latter of thefe being the more Charitable Conjecture of the two, it will be *the more allowable to lay the Blame of the Mifcarriage there: However, I will endeavour (as far as I am able) to apply a Remedy to both ·in this prefent Paper; Wherein my defign is, to give a brief and plain Expofition of this great Law of Nature, and of the Gofpel. And although a Difcourfe of this Nature may feem a little out of Fafhion, and Alien to the humor of the prefent Times; yet (befides that I hope the Brevity may in fome meafure Attone for the

the Unfafhionablenefs) I am per-
fwaded that (all things duly confidered) there is hardly any thing
elfe (which may be comprized in fo
little Room) can be done more
feafonably for the Age we live in,
or whereby one can exprefs more
good Will to all Mankind in general.

Therefore I will proceed in this
Method :

1. I will plainly lay open the ge-
nuine Meaning of this Rule.

2. I will fhew the Natural and
Univerfal Equity of it.

3. I will defcribe the juft Bounds
and Limits of its Obligation.

4. I will fpecific fome of the
Cafes which it Over-rules and
Determines.

And

And then Laftly, For a Conclufion, I will reprefent the happy
Effects and Advantages of Li-
ving and Acting accordingly.

1. *For the Explication of this
Rule.*

Towards the underftanding of
this *Aphorifm*, there is nothing more
requifite to be fuppofed, than (that
which cannot be doubted or denyed,
namely,) That there is fuch a Principle in us as *Self-Love*. And this
(confidered in it felf) is not only
innocent and allowable, but ufeful
and neceffary: For it is not the Iffue
of the Corruption and Depravation
of our Nature, but implanted in us
by our Creator for great and wife
Purpofes, partly to be a Guard and
Prefervative of our Beings; partly
to fweeten our Lives to us; but
principally to be the Foundation of
all his Laws, or at leaft the great
Engine by which He moves and
governs

The Golden Rule. 7

governs us. For by this Handle of
our *Self-Love* God Almighty takes
hold of us; by this Helm he turns
us about agreeably to his own
Defigns: For it is evident, that if
we had no delight in our Selves, no
tendernefs for our own Concerns, it
would be to no effect to propound
Laws to us, and to back them
with the Threatnings and Promifes
of Rewards and Punifhments; and
confequently it would be only in
the Power of the Almighty to de-
ftroy us, (if he pleafed) but impoffible to govern us.

Now that which is peculiar to
the Cafe in hand is this, That
whereas in all other Inftances of
our Duty towards G O D, this
Principle of *Self-Love* is (as I faid
before) only an Hank upon us, or
the Motive of our Obedience.
Now here in this Law *of Loving
our Neighbour*, it is not only the
Motive, but the Rule and Meafure
alfo of our Duty. So that hereby
we

we have a ready Way to refolve our Selves of the Manner of our Carriage; and all our Actions towards others. For GOD having made it our Duty in the General, to Love our Neighbour as our Self; there is then no more to be done, but to turn our Eye inward, and confult that *Urim* and *Thummim* in our own Breafts, and we are prefently inftructed in all the Particulars of that Duty. Neither is there any need we fhould trouble our Selves to confult *Books* or *Philofophers*, or *Lawyers* or *Cafuifts*, having a ftanding Oracle in our own Bofoms, which will as certainly determine us.

This is a Standard which can never fail us, till we Defert or can Hate our Selves, which is impoffible.

And

And it is a full and sufficient Standard too ; for no Man will be Niggardly toward himself, and if I give other Men the same Measure I use to my Self, there can be no cause of Complaint.

And it is as easie and plain, and ready at hand, as it is full and certain; for it is but turning the *Tables*, and supposing my Case to be my Neighbours, or his to be Mine, and my Way is plain before me. It is possible I may Envy my Neighbour, and that may tempt me to give a wrong Judgment; but then do but change the Scales, and put Him in my place and my Self in his, and I cannot but be impartial: For though I have a Prejudice against Him, I have none against my Self. It is possible also, That my Neighbour may be greedy, and unreasonably desire of me more than is fit; but to decide the Point, let me but put my self in his stead, and

and bethink my felf what I fhould judge then equal for me to defire of Him; and fo much and no more is due from Me to Him. Moreover, when Men are in Profperity, there is nothing more common than for fuch to Contemn and Browbeat thofe that are in Adverfity; and on the other fide, it is as ordinary for Men in Adverfity to Envy and Malign, and Cenfure thofe in Profperity. Now to difcover the Evil of both thofe, and withal to gain to our Selves a Rule of our Carriage in either Cafe, let the *Tables* be turned, and for the prefent fuppofe the Rich Man to be the Poor Man, and the Poor Man to become the Rich; and then we fhall fee what is fit on both fides. For moft certainly, if this Rich Man was put in the Scale of the Poor, he would think it very hard to be defpifed meerly becaufe he is Poor, and to have his Calamity imputed to him as his Crime, or his Folly; but would think it

Juft

Juſt (for all that difference of Condition) that he ſhould be kindly and
humanly Treated in his Adverſity.
On the other ſide, Put the Poor
Man into the Rich Mans place and
he would aſſuredly think, that
though a Man is not always the
wiſer or better Man for being Rich;
yet there is ſome Reſpect due to his
Place and Quality; and he would
not think he deſerved to be called
a Proud Man meerly for keeping
up his Port and Character; and
thus both Parties judge right and
ſpeak Truth in their own Caſe, that
could not diſcern it in anothers.
And thus we ſee the uſe of an
Appeal to this Principle of *Self-
Love*, and that in ſo doing we have
a *Chancery* and Court of Equity
in our own Boſoms. And ſo we
have the meaning of this Rule,
which was the firſt thing pro-
pounded.

2. Now

2. *Now Secondly, For the Equity
and Natural Obligation of this
Rule.*

This will appear upon a double
Account, *viz.* partly from the
actual Equality of Nature in all
Men, and partly from the Possibility and Probability of Equality
of Condition in all Men, one time
or other.

First, It is naturally fit and rea-
sonable, that we should carry an
Even hand between our selves and
other Men, *and Love our Neighbour
as our Self*, forasmuch as he is properly as our self, there being an
actual Equality of Nature in all
Men : For whatsoever difference
there may happen to be in mens
outward Circumstances, all That is
but Accidental, and when they are
considered as divested of those
Circumstances, they are all substan-
tially alike. All have the same
Creator,

Creator, and stand in the same Relation to God; all Mens Bodies were made out of the same Earth, and (as it were) cast in the same Mold; they are all born alike, and dye alike: And for their Souls, they are equal too, all have the same Divine Image upon them, the same Faculties, and Reason is the same throughout the World. Consequently of this they are all common Citizens of the World, and (as to Nature) have an equal share in it. Now *æqualibus æqualia tribuere*, to deal alike between those that are equal in themselves, is a first Principle of Reason in all Mankind, and therefore to deal by our Neighbour as we would be dealt by our selves, is an universal and indispensable Law of Justice.

Secondly, There is a possibility, if not a probability of the equality of all mens Conditions and

Circumstances one time or other;
he that is now rich may be poor,
and he that is poor may become rich; the Man of Dignity
and Power may be depressed,
and the mean Man may be ex-
alted ; and such Changes are so
frequent , that he must be prodi-
giously vain and stupid, that doth
not apprehend it may be his own
Case at one time or other ; and
if he be apprehensive of such a
vicissitude of things , he will have
all the reason in the World to
provide for it accordingly, that is,
if he now be on the advantage
Ground , he will yet be humble,
and modest , and merciful towards
his Inferiours , and those in Adversity : And if he be now at
the bottom , he will hope his
Condition may mend, and in the
mean time think such thoughts of
those above him , as he would be
willing should be entertained concerning himself when the tyde is
turned.

turned. And he that doth not so,
is neither just for the present,
nor provident for the future; for
he hath no certain measure of
his Actions, but goes by a Rule
now, which he would be loath to
stand to at another time. And so
much for that; I proceed to shew

3. *The just Bounds and Limits of
this Axiom.*

However easie and expedite this
Rule may seem to be (by what
we have hitherto said) yet it is
notoriously certain, That there are
very great and frequent Mistakes
in the Application of it, whilst
some take it in so large a sense
as to supersede all other Laws,
both Humane and Divine, by it;
and others as much restraining
and straitening the Scope of it,
make it indeed no Rule at all,
but a bare Saying to serve a
turn by now and then. There-
B 2   fore

fore I think it neceſſary, befor
I proceed in the Deduction of
Practical Conſequences from this
Axiom, to lay down the follow-
ing Particulars for the more full
Explication of it. And

Firſt, It is to be conſidered,
That this Rule or Aphoriſm before us, is only intended for the
Government of our Actions towards Men, not for a Meaſure
of Religion (properly ſo called)
or of our Carriage towards God.
For he being infinite in all Per-
ſections, there is nothing in us
that we can appeal to as a Meaſure of what is due towards
him. Neither is it enough for us
to love God as we love our
ſelves, for he being infinitely better than our ſelves, it is conſe-
quently our duty to love him
better than we love our ſelves,
namely with all our heart, and
ſoul, and ſtrength; and if more
than

than that was poffible to be per-
formed by us, it would be due
to him accordingly. But now it
is fufficient that I love my Neighbour as my felf, becaufe (as I
have fhewed) he is like my felf,
or a kind of fecond felf, and it
would be a kind of Injuftice to
love him better than my felf,
becaufe then I do not *æqualibus
æqualia tribuere*. And confequently I cannot be naturally bound
to dye for my Neighbour, becaufe this fuppofes that I ought
to love him better than my felf.
But on the other fide, I am
bound (if occafion be, and when
God's Honour requires it) to dye
for God, becaufe he is infinitely
better than my felf. and therefore is to be preferr'd before my
Life, or whatfoever elfe is dear-
eft to me.

B 3   This

This I think is plain enough, and needed not to have been said here, but for the sake of some conceited Moralists (as they love to be called) who shrink up all Religion into this one Precept *of doing as they would be done unto*; as if this was not only the whole Decalogue, but their Creed and *Pater noster* too. And for countenance of this absurd Perfwasion, they insist upon those words which *our Saviour adds as an *Encomium* of the Maxim aforesaid, *For this is the Law and the Prophets*, as if this one Saying comprehended the whole Doctrine of the Old and New Testament.

But it is very plain that those latter words of our Saviour ought not, nor can be so loosly understood ; for to imagine him to affert that this one great Maxim exprest the whole Duty of Man,

is

is to fuppofe him to make void all Divine Revelation , and to take away all neceffity either of Old or New Teftament , forafmuch as this Rule is clear enough of it felf by the meer Light of Nature, and accordingly hath been acknowledged by thofe that never had any other Light to guide them , as we have intimated already.

Befides , Man is not our only Correlative , but * we ftand in Relation to a God that made us, as well as to Man that is made like us, and therefore the greateft and higheft part of our Duty refults from that higher Relation, and thofe greater Obligations we have upon us towards God , than towards one another. In Contemplation of which a Heathen could fay , *Quid aliud eft Pietas quam Juftitia adverfus Deos*; that Piety is Juftice, and that neglect

B 4   of

of Religious obfervance of the Divine Majefty is as manifeft Injuftice towards him, as any inftance of Fraud or Violence towards our Neighbour can amount unto.

The meaning therefore of our Saviour in thofe additional words, *This is the Law and the Prophets,* can be no more but this, *viz.* That the Rule aforefaid is the fum of the Second Table of the Law, and of the Expofitions and Paraphrafes of the Prophets upon it. For accordingly we obferve in a parallel place, *Matth.* 22. 36. when a Lawyer asks this Queftion, *Mafter, which is the great Commandment of the Law:* Our Saviour anfwers, *Thou fhalt love the Lord thy God with all thy Heart, and with all thy Soul, and with all thy Mind; this is the firft and great Commandment: And the fecond is like unto it, namely,*
Thou

Thou shalt love thy Neighbour as thy self: And then adds, *On these two hang all the Law and the Prophets.* Where we see, beyond all dispute, that the whole Model of our Duty, nor the intire design of the Law and Prophets, is not comprized in one of these Rules, but in both together.

Secondly, It is further considerable, That even in relation to our Neighbour, and in the conduct and government of our Actions towards Men, this Maxim is rather to be looked upon as a Measure than a Law properly so called: My meaning is, That the use of it is rather to prescribe to us how much we should do, than what we should do, or as that which rather determines the proportion of our Actions, than justifies the matter of them. To speak more plainly yet, (if it be possible) I say this Rule is intended

tended principally to direct us
what Meafures we are to take,
and what Proportion to obferve,
in the Difcharge of fuch an Action towards our Neighbour, where
and when the Action or Thing
it felf in the general is already
known to be certainly lawful;
not for a Law properly to warrant the thing we are about,
whatfoever it is. For if it was
otherwife, a common Drunkard
might juftifie his indeavour of debauching other Men into that
beaftly Vice, under this pretence,
That he doth nothing in that
cafe, but what he is content
fhould be done to himfelf. And
the Lafcivious perfon, fo he might
be allowed to defile his Neighbours
Bed, would perhaps be content
another fhould do as much for
him. And no queftion but a dex-
terous Cheat would allow others
to cheat him if they could, provided he might exercife his Ta-
lent

lent that way without controle.

Therefore (as I said) this Axiom doth not priviledge evil Actions, no nor so much as determine any Action to be good meerly upon the reciprocal inclination of mens minds. For this were at once to repeal all the Laws of God and Man, and under pretence of making every man a Law to himself, to make him absolutely lawless: But it only prescribes the meassure of our Actions *in materiâ licita & honesta.*

For example; Suppose I am in deliberation with my self, how I ought to carry my self towards my poor Brother in his Adversity, and what Relief I am bound to give him, or how far I ought to strain my self in his Case. Here now I am certain that the thing I deliberate about is lawful and good in the general; and then
this

this Rule comes feafonably in for my direction in the meafure of my Performance, *viz.* It tells me that I am to deal by that poor man, juft as I would be dealt with by him, if his Cafe were mine, and mine were his. But now on the other fide, Suppofe the thing I am deliberating about, be the retaliating of an Injury, or the revenging my felf upon him that hath done me wrong; Here now I muft firft fee a Law juftifying me in revenging my felf, before I can refolve my felf of the meafure of Revenge which I am to take. For it will not be a fufficient Warrant to me, that I intend to proceed equitably, or that I will do by that man only juft as in like Cafe I would be content to be done unto. But I muft firft be fure that it is lawful for me to revenge my felf, and that I do not break another Law, ufurping God's Prerogative, who

who hath told us *Vengeance is his.*

Thirdly, Moreover if this Bufineſs be well confidered, we ſhall find that this Maxim is not abſolutely a Rule *in materiâ licitâ & honeſta* neither, but only *in re debitâ.* My meaning is, That to apply this Maxim to its peculiar uſe and intent, we muſt not only be ſatisfied antecedently, that the Matter of the Action we are about be in it ſelf lawful, (without which we have ſeen already that *to do as we would be done by* will not bear us out) but it is alſo required that that very Meaſure of that Thing or Action which this Rule obliges me to obſerve towards my Neighbour, be ſuch as I ſhould think was due and of right belonging to me, if the Caſe was mine, as it is now another mans. For I am not bound to do to another

other all that which it is lawful for him to do to me, no,
nor all that which I could wish
he should do to me; nor on the
other side am I bound to refrain
from doing to him that which
I could heartily wish he should
refrain from doing to me; but
my Obligation from this Rule
principally lies in this, that I
both do, or refrain from doing
(respectively) towards him, all that
which (turning the Tables and then
consulting my own Heart and
Conscience) I should think that
Neighbour of mine *bound* to do,
or to refrain from doing towards
me in the like Case.

As for Example; If I was in
extreme Poverty, when my Neighbour was in as great Afflu-
ence and Prosperity, no doubt
but I should be easily tempted
to wish, That he out of his A-
bundance should not only re-
lieve

lieve my prefent and urgent Neceffity, or fupply me from
Hand to Mouth (as we fay) but
alfo that he fhould pour out his
Surplufage upon me, and once for
all by a great Effort of Charity,
put me quite out of my diftref-
fed Condition. This, I fay, I
could wifh in my own Cafe ; and
there is no doubt but that it is
in it felf lawful for fuch a Rich
man as aforefaid, fo to do if he
pleafes ; yet for all this I cannot
think him bound fo to do, or
that he fins if he doth not fo;
for I cannot find that if the Tables were turned, I fhould think
it to be a fin in my felf not to
do fo by him; and therefore it
cannot be a Duty in him to do
fo by me.

Again, It may be I could wifh
that fome Laws of the Land were
more accommodate to my convenience, and it is poffible the Law-
maker

maker might have contrived, things
more for my convenience, without any fin or fault on his part;
yet fo long as thofe Laws are
juft in themfelves, and fuited to
the Publick Good, I cannot think
it the Duty of the Supreme Magiftrate fo far to confult my particular Intereft; for (turning the Tables) I fhould not have thought it
to have been my own Duty in
fuch a Cafe, therefore I ought in
that Cafe not to complain, but
in all reafon to fubmit my private Intereft to that of the Publick.

I will give one Example more
(becaufe this Point is a little
obfcure and difficult to be right-
ly explained otherwife than by
Inftances). It is certain that a-
ny Man would be loath to be
put to death as a Malefactor,
whatever the Cafe or his Deme-
rit fhall be: And I think I may
take

take it for granted that there are
feveral Cafes wherein the Prince
or Supreme Magiftrate may pardon if he pleafe, though the
Malefactor juftly deferve Death;
Now fure it would be very ab-
furd to conclude from hence,
that therefore he ought to pardon
me in fuch a Cafe, or to fay
that he is cruel in putting me
to death, which I have otherwife deferved: For though I could
wifh for a Pardon, and he hath
it in his power to give it me,
yet it will not follow that he fins
if he do not; for my own Heart
doth not tell me that I was *bound*
to do fo in the like Cafe; and
therefore if I make the fame Meafure ferve for both Parties, I
cannot (according to the Rule
before us) pronounce that he *ought*
to do fo.

C. Not

The Golden Rule.

Not therefore whatfoever I
could honeſtly enough wiſh for
at the hands of my Neighbour,
nor every thing that it is lawful
for him to do , is neceſſary to
be done to me , but only that
which I can reaſonably judge
(turning the Tables that ſo I may
be impartial) to be the Duty of
my Neighbour towards me , and
that becauſe I ſhould think it to
be my Duty towards him in the
like Caſe, that is to be the Meaſure of my Expectations from
him , and I may juſtly challenge
that , and no more from him ,
upon this Rule of Equity.

Thus much hath been ſaid hitherto , to prevent the ſtraining
of this Rule beyond the true reaſon and intent of it. Now to
provide againſt the like Miſtakes
on the other hand , and to give it
its true *Scope* and Latitude, I add
two Particulars more, *viz.*

Fourth-

Fourthly then, It is to be considered, That as all men are equal in Nature (as we shewed before) and consequently whatsoever Treatment is due to one Man, must be so to another; Therefore this same Rule is to govern all Men in all their Actions and Intercourse one with another, without partiality or respect of Persons, of what Condition or Quality soever they be. For this is a Rule, not an Advice only, not a Thing which we may do well to observe, but matter of Law and Duty upon all Men. And therefore the *Prince* is obliged by it as well as Private men; for this being founded in primary Nature, is antecedent to all the several Ranks and Distinctions of Men. *It is* a Rule between Men of several Countries and Dominions, as well as between Neighbours; for our Saviour

C 2   hath

hath shewed us that all Mankind are to be esteemed our Neighbours. *It is* to be observed between Men of several Religions, as well as those that are of the same way of Worship; nay the same equitable Carriage is due to the Men of the most abject and senseless Opinions, as to those of the truest and most excellent Profession; for Mens weakness and folly (or whatever we impute their Errours to) destroys not their Natural Right to an equitable usage.

It is true amongst the People of the *Jews*, there was an Exception in this Case, and they were not bound to do to all Men as they would be done unto; for God (by a peculiar Dispensation) having condemned the Seven Nations to utter Destruction, had exempted them from the common Priviledges of Mankind: And besides,

besides his Divine Wisdom (having a design to separate the People of the *Jews* from all Nations of the Earth) not only instituted peculiar Rites for the distinction of this People from all others, but also (in pursuance of that end) allowed and required they should in some respect, treat all other People as Strangers. But when our Saviour came, that Wall of Partition was pulled down, and all the World were made one People; and from that time especially this Rule of Universal Equity takes place without Exception. And now no Man can be so inconsiderable, or of so despicable a Condition, but he hath an Interest in the Common Charity of Christians: No Man so remote from us in his Country or Habitation, or so different from us in Opinion, or so silly in his Understanding, or so vicious in his Manners, or so ill

tem-

temper'd for his Nature, but there
is a common Tye of Equity between us and him, which no mis-
carriage of his can forfeit, nor a-
ny Power on Earth can difpenfe
with. And therefore thofe that
now confine Equity and Juftice,
and Charity to a Party, that
imagine they can do no Wrong
to a Diffenter, that fancy no Faith
is to be kept with Hereticks, or
the like, they revive the very
Dregs of Judaifm, and utterly de-
ftroy the great Defign of Chriftianity, whilft they are ignorantly
zealous of their own Opinions.

Fifthly and Laftly, It is to be
obferved, That this Paffage of our
Saviour's was not intended fo
much to be a Rule of Retribution
or Requital, as of Kindnefs and
primary Obligation. For it is not
faid., *Do to other Men as they do
or have done to you; but as ye
would they fhould do to you* That is,

As

As if our Saviour had said, I would
have my Diſciples ſo prompt, and
ſo inclined to good Offices towards each other, that I would
not have them ſtay till an Obligation is laid upon them, and
that then they ſhould requite it
with the like: But I would have
Chriſtians anticipate, begin, and
be an Example of Kindneſs to
one another, or to make Prece-
dents and Inſtances of Beneficence
where they find none, and ſo
bring the World to be better na-
tured. In a word, To *do that to
others in the firſt place, which they
would be glad to receive from o-
thers in the ſecond place.* This,
(I take it) is to interpret this
Rule properly in an Evangelical
Senſe; for this is the peculiar Spirit of the Goſpel, to oblige the Pro-
feſſors of it to be the Salt of
the Earth, the Light of the
World, and the firſt Movers in
every good thing. And to that

pur-

purpose it requires *We should love our Enemies, do good to them that hate us and persecute us. Not to be overcome of Evil, but to overcome Evil with Good*; i. e.by Kindness and Beneficence to melt Men into good Nature : Which I think is the meaning of that Phrase of the Apostle, who tells us, by so doing *We shall heap Coals of Fire on their Heads.*

It is a brutish thing to think our selves licensed to do Evil to others, because they have done so ro us. It is a Pharisaical thing to do Good only in proportion to what is done to us ; and it is a selfish stingy thing to do it upon that Motive, and in Expectation that it may be so done to us; but the temper of a Christian is to do good without invitation or provocation from the meer Benignity of his Nature, and out of meer Love of Beneficence ; and then

for

for the proportion of that Beneficence, that is to be fo great, as
what we would gladly meet with
from others, if the Cafe was alter'd.

4. *I come now , as the fourth
part of this fhort Difcourfe ,
to fpecifie fome of the principal Cafes which this Axiom
(fo interpreted as aforefaid)
will over-rule and determine ,
and confequently to fhew of
what great Influence it will be
upon Human Affairs , if it be
applyed accordingly.*

And indeed the Ufe of this
Rule is fo general, and the Oc-
cafions of having recourfe to it ,
are fo frequent , that Experience
only can moft effectually fhew the
Importance of it. However, Since
I am obliged to inftance in fome
Particulars , I will fpecifie thefe
following (as they come to my
thoughts) without being over
care-

careful of the Order in which I
fet them down.

Firſt, The attending to this one
Rule before us, would in a great
meaſure prevent the Wars and
Bloodſhed that are in the World,
and therewithal would hinder that
Cruelty and Rapine, thoſe Deſola-
tions of Countries, and Convulſi-
ons of Kingdoms, which are not
more the Infelicities, than the
Shame and Reproach of Mankind.
And which almoſt as much take
away the diſtinction between Man
and Beaſt; as they deſtroy the
Bleſſings and Comfort of Human
Life.

I know the common pretence
for War is, That between Soveraign Princes and States, there are
no Common Tribunals to decide
the Controverſies, and therefore
it is ſaid there is a Neceſſity of
Appealing to the great Soveraign
of

of the World, *The Lord of Hosts.*
But is there no such thing as a
Court of Conscience or Common
Equity? Is there no Common-
Law of Reason? Are there no
General Bonds of Human Socie-
ty? Is there no such Universal
Rule, as to *do as we would be
done by?*

If there be none, then the
Sword may Ravage the World,
Jusque datum sceleri, and the greatest Force hath the best Cause.
But if there be (as we have shewed there is) then the considerati-
on of it; and application to it,
might end Disputes without the
Umpirage of the Sword; for then
Princes will be concerned in it as
well as Subjects; forasmuch as
when they put on the Diadem,
they do not put off the Men.
And then it will not seem war-
rantable to involve whole Nations
in Blood upon a *Punctilio* of Honour,

nour, or for the Glory of their own Name, or for Increase of Territory; or in a word, for what they can get. It will not then seem lawful to Invade another's Dominions, because that Prince is weak and unprovided; or to take Advantage of Inteſtine Diviſions, or the Minority of the Prince, or the Corruption of his Miniſters, or other Difficulties he labours under. For whoſoever looks home will readily acknowledge, That he would not be ſo dealt with himſelf, and therefore ought to uſe the ſame Meaſure towards others. For (though *Inter arma ſilent Leges*, yet) the Court of Conſcience is always open, Equity hath no Non-Term, written Laws may be interrupted, but this *Lex non ſcripta ſed nata* is always of force.

It

It is said the Turks, before they ingage in a War, are wont to consult their great *Mufti* or *High-Priest* about the lawfulness of the Enterprise. And the Pagans of old used solemnly to advise with their Oracles in such Cases: And even amongst Christians a Consecrated Sword, or an Hallowed Banner from the chief Pontiff, uses to incourage the Expedition. But without that Ceremony and Pomp, here is an Oracle in our own Breast, which if Men would consult ingenuously, it would for the most part dissuade the War; or if it did not, it would marvellously tend to succeed the Prosecution. It would (I say) ordinarily be like to *Socrates* his *Genius* or *Good Angel*, which was observed by himself generally to Caution and Restrain him, but seldom or never to prompt or inflame him. Which, I remember
Tully

Tully faith, is no more than the constant *Genius* of every Wise man.

And if it shall happen that Wars be undertaken without asking the Counsel of this Oracle, (as too commonly they are) and withal be successful too, (which frequently they are not) yet the Injustice will blemish the Glory of the Victory: For even amongst the *Romans*, nothing more frequent in their own Histories, than to lay a Blot upon such Atchievements. So *Florus* leaves upon Record, *Cretici Belli nullam aliam fuisse Causam, quam Nobilis-Insulæ acquirendæ cupiditatem:* It was Covetousness, and not Justice, that moved that War. And to the same purpose *Ammianus Marcellinus*, speaking of the Enterprize upon *Cyprus*, faith, *Cypram insulam avidè magis, quam justè Populum Romanum invasisse.* And to name no more, *Petronius Arbiter*

Arbiter hath blasted almost all the Glory of the Roman Arms in these few words;

——*Si quis sinus abditus ultrà,*
Si qua foret Tellus quæ fulvum mit-
teret aurum,
Hostis erat, &c.

So that it seems, even amongst that grasping and warlike Nation, there was an apprehension of the Obligation of Equity and Justice towards other People, and that they did not think that every thing was lawful to him that had the longest Sword. And therefore though this apprehension was not always sufficient to restrain their Covetousness and Ambition, yet it ought to have done, and shamed them when it did not.

But *Secondly*, If Princes and great States be not to be restrain-ed by this Law, and Force must

be

be the *Ratio ultima Regum*, yet sure amongst private Persons it may be attended to, and be of Authority enough to suppress Duels, and *the shedding of the Blood of War In Peace*, as the Scripture calls it; which is the most Savage and Belluine Custom that can be imagined, and so much worse than War it self, in that that hath some excuse, (as I intimated before) *viz.* because between Soveraign Princes there is no Superiour Court to Appeal to for Justice; whereas in this Case there is a Remedy in Human Judicatures: But especially it is intolerable that the Life of my Neighbour, and my own too, should be put upon the Point of the Sword, on the slightest Provocations, for a contumelious Expression which a Wise man would despise; nay, it may be, for a meer rash Word, or a Jest, which a great minded Man would not think worth his Animadversion.

madverſion. Now if Men conſul-
ted their own Reaſon, or Conſcience, or any thing, but meerly
their Brutiſh Paſſion in ſuch Caſes, would they not make Allowance for ſuch Follies and In-
advertencies in others? ſince they
are not exempted from them, themſelves : Would they be contented
to anſwer with their Lives for e-
very Indiſcretion they have been
Guilty of? If they can be ſo content, they are unworthy of Life
who value it at ſo mean a rate:
If they cannot, they confeſs themſelves to proceed unjuſtly. But
above all, why ſhould not a Man
in ſuch a Caſe take his Meaſures
from the fifth Particular in the
Explication of this Rule, and take
a Chriſtian and a Noble Revenge
indeed; that is, Why ſhould he
not forgive the Injury, and ſo be
above his Adverſary? the other
way, at beſt, I put my ſelf but
upon the Level with him; but
           D   here

here I place my self above him,
and triumph over him. Why
should I not oblige him by Kindness, and heap Coals of Fire
on his Head, and rather, like a
brave Christian, do that which
I wish he had done to me; than
like a Beast, hurt him because he
hath hurt me?

Thirdly, The Application of
this Rule to our Practises, would
tend very much to the preventi-
on of another Evil, not much in-
feriour to either of the former,
namely Law-Suits, which in truth
are but another kind of War,
and are usually managed with as
much Malice and Rancour as War
it self. Certainly they are a great
Reproach to Christendom, and to
this Nation in particular. It is an
unhappy Observation (of some
Body) *That what the Moors spend*
at the Jollities of their Weddings,
the Jews at the Solemnity of their
Passover,

Paſſover, that and more the Chri-
ſtians expend in Law-Suits. And
it is verily thought that the whole
Expence of Law in *England*, is e-
qual to the Charge of a Foreign
War. But it is not only the Expence of Mony that is deplora-
ble in this Caſe, but the imbroy-
ling Mens Spirits, the inflaming
their Paſſions, the hinderance and
ſcandal to Religion, and the in-
tailing of Quarrels upon Poſterity.
Now if theſe things were fatally
neceſſary and unavoidable, it were
in vain to complain and aggravate
the matter; but there is a Remedy at hand, if we would make
uſe of it: Time hath been when
it was otherwiſe, and therefore
it may be ſo again. *What* (ſaith
the Apoſtle 1 *Cor.* 6. 5.) *is there
not a Wiſe man amongſt you ? no
not one that ſhall be able to judge
between his Brethren ?* But eſpeci-
ally is there no ſuch thing as
Conſcience of Equity ? Have we

not a Judge within us? Is not
this Law before us sufficient to
determine our Quarrels? Let but
the Plaintiff put himself in the
Case of the Defendant, and the
Defendant suppose himself in the
place of the Plaintiff, and both
shall easily see what is fit to be
done, and Matters will be amica-
bly composed.

Fourthly, The Observation of
this Rule would as well advance
the Interest and Reputation of the
Christian Church, as the Quiet
of the World ; for it would at
once both prevent most of those
Severities that Christians too frequently use one towards another
upon the account of Religion, and
also put a stop to the Clamours
upon that Occasion. It is undeni-
ably true, That very hard things
have been done upon the Score of
Propagating or Preserving the Truth
and Purity of Religion. And it is

as

as true, That very great Noises and Complaints have been made of Perfecution, when perhaps there hath been no juſt Cauſe for it. And there is hardly to be found any great Party of Men that can clearly waſh their Hands of both theſe Miſcarriages, and few that can quit themſelves of either of them : For it hath too ordinarily happened, That the ſame Perſons who have at one time been too unchriſtianly harſh toward others, have at another time been as blameably too tender and ſenſible when the Tyde hath been turned, and it is become their own Caſe: Forgetting in the former Inſtance to do as they would be done unto; and not conſidering in the other Inſtance, That if what they did before was juſt towards others, it ought not to be Matter of Complaint when it comes home to themſelves.

There

There is no doubt but there is a vast difference between these two things, and that it is far better to complain unjustly, than to do cruelly ; yet neither are to be excused : For as by the former, *viz.* Exclaiming of Persecution without just Ground, not only a general Odium is kindled against those that out of Zeal pursue those severe Methods; but oftentimes the State and Civil Government is indanger'd by the Flames kindled thereupon: So by the latter, (I mean Persecution properly so called) Religion it self is made odious, and loses its principal Glory of being Rational, and commending it self by its own Light ; and Men are tempted to suspect that to be destitute of good proof, which needs to be supported by Force, and (so like Colours in the dark) all Religions are alike, when the use of Reason is laid aside, and

Force

Force supplies the room of it. And consequently all study and ingenuous ways of improving Mens minds are superseded; for where it is become the fashion to knock Men on the Head that will not be Converted, it will not seem worth the while to take the pains to convince them. And in short, the very temper of Religion it self, will in time be supplanted, and only a dull sottish Compliance upon implicit Faith, and a formal Hypocrisie succeed in the room of it.

But now (as I said) both these Mischiefs may be avoided by a due Application of the Maxim before us : For on the one side, As for those blind Zealots that are always most fierce and forward in Persecution, though they have little or no Conscience, yet they cannot be without this Principle of Self-love ; and though they have not Judgment to discern the diffe-

D 4   rence

rence of things, yet they may turn the Tables and change the Scale, and see how things look on both sides.

As for Example ; I would fain have another Man be of my Opinion , yet sure it will not look well to knock him on the Head if he be not : For, turning the Tables, I find that I would not be so dealt with in the like Case : Especially seeing he is a Man , and I am no more ; and consequently I am no more infallible than he is; and therefore he hath as much right to persecute me into his Opinion , as I have to force him into mine.

Or suppose I would be glad that the way I am of, should be incouraged , and the contrary discouraged , but however it will not be fit to starve all those that dissent from it; for I should think it great Cruelty to be so dealt with my self.   But

But it may be, the way I am of, is that which hath publick Allowance, and is reputed the moſt Orthodox: yet if I look into my ſelf, I find that I cannot be of what Opinion I will : And if it was my Fortune to be Heterodox, I ſhould think it hard to be rackt up to the Publick Standard; therefore ſuch Uſage cannot be equal towards other Men.

But perhaps ſome Man will ſay, Are then all Opinions alike? Is there no Advantage to be given to Truth above Errour? Is not the one to be propagated with all our might, and the other to be as carefully ſuppreſſed? I anſwer, Yes doubtleſs; there is a very different treatment due to Truth than to Errour, provided we be ſure which is which. For otherwiſe, one Man is apt to be as confident of his Perſwaſion, as another Man can be be of his ; therefore it is fit that Infallible Wisdom should determine between them , and that can be no otherwise done than by the plain and exprefs Letter of Holy Scripture. ·Without this Umpirage we may indulge our own Fancies and Paffions under a Notion of Zeal of God and Truth. But if there be plain and exprefs Scripture in the Cafe , then (though it always becomes a Chriftian to incline to the fide of Tendernefs and Mercy, yet) for my part (till I am better informed) I fhall not call it Perfecution to make a great difference in the Countenance and Incouragement I give to that which is fo warranted. And if this was not true, then it would follow that whenfoever I meet with any Severities made ufe of in the Holy Scripture in the Cafe of Religion (of which we have frequent Inftances in the Old Teftament efpecially) I muft call that alfo a Culpable Perfecution : which

which I am sure I ought not to do. But if it come to this Point, and all Persecution be stopt, but where the Truth is defined expresly by God himself, the first Mischief is cured (for ought I know) as far as it ought to be.

On the other side , as for those querulous Persons who are apt to complain before they are hurt, and to scandalize the Laws, and reflect on their Governours, under the Notion of Persecution, their Noise would be stilled if they attended to this Rule of Equity , and doing as they would be done to. It is true, I would have my Conscience to my self, and think it horribly tyrannical , that any Body should impose upon me to believe as he pleases. But on the other side, If I must have my own Opinion , must I have my Will too? Must I be uppermost in the State? and be put in Power and Authority equal with

with other Men , or elſe I am
perſecuted? Nay, muſt I not only
enjoy my own Conſcience , but
affront other Mens, or elſe I am
rigorouſly dealt with ? Muſt I have
liberty to ſcorn and blaſpheme another Religion , or elſe I am not
ſuffered comfortably to enjoy my
own? In a word, Is my Birthright
violated , and my Natural Liberty
of chooſing my own Religion in-
fringed , if the Publick Religion of
the Country , and that which is
eſtabliſhed by the Laws, be incouraged by the Advantages of
Publick Maintenance ? Surely theſe
are very extravagant Collections ,
and any Man that turns the Tables, will eaſily diſcern them to be
ſo, and to contain more of Humour
than Conſcience; for whatſoever
Allowance I ought to make in fa-
vour of Liberty and Conſcience ,
yet reflecting upon my ſelf impar-
tially , I am certain that if my
Religion was the Publick Eſtabliſh-
                                    ment,

ment, I should think somewhat the more respect due to it upon that account: And if I was then in Authority (though I would deprive no man of his Natural Rights for not complying with the Publick Opinion, yet) I would be sure to incourage and prefer those that thought and professed as I did; nay, it may be I should proceed so far, as to put some Mark of distinction upon those that did not so. And I should be so far from pulling down those Fences or Outworks which the Wisdom of my Ancestors had provided for the Security of that Religion which I was perswaded was the Truth, that I would not stick to restrain (by some fit Punishments) those Insolent People who could not be content with their own Liberty, without affronting mine and the established Religion. And all this I should not doubt to do without incurring the odious Name of a *Persecutor.*

Perfecutor. And theretore fince I fhould think it lawful to do all this , were the Cafe my own, *viz.* That I was on the advantage Ground , and had the Laws on my fide : I cannot with any colour of Reafon complain if thus much , and no more , be done to me when I am on the wrong fide of the Hedge, and maintain only a private and difallowed Opinion.

Again *Fifthly* , The framing of our felves by this Rule of doing as, *&c.* would produce another Temper and Spirit than is commonly feen in the Age we live in , efpecially in the managing of Difputes and Controverfies in Religion , whether by way of private Conference , or publick Writings. The Heats and Paffions , the Taunts and Scorns, and Contumelious Treatments of one another in thefe Affairs, are fcandalous

dalous to a Proverb, *Odium Theolo-*
gorum. Men not only fill up the
void Places or Intervals of their
Difcourfes with Reproaches, but
blot both fides of their Paper with
fuch filthy ftuff.

Now I will not only fay that
this Carriage is utterly unbecom-
ing Chriftianity, which requires
and produces (wherever it prevails
effectually) the moft Mild, Innocent, and Dove-like. Temper: Nor
will I fay only that this kind of
Management is moft peculiarly un-
decent in fo grave and folemn an
Affair as Religion is: But that
which I would fay is, That who-
foever confults his own Breaft,
would never be guilty of this
Fault towards any fort of men,
fince he will find there, That he
would not be dealt with fo himfelf. I know my Adverfary thinks
otherwife than I do; but why may
not he think as well as I; or
how

how far do I differ from him,
more than he doth from me? I
am content therefore he should
urge me with his Reasons, because
I would do so by him: But in-
stead of hard Arguments, I would
not have him pelt me with hard
Words; and therefore I ought not
to do so by him. Let him stick
upon the Merits of the Cause,
but not blemish my Person or
Reputation. I take it to be a
sign a Man is destitute of good
Proofs, when *furor arma ministrat*,
and when Passion supplies the
place of Reason; and if it be so in
another, it is no better in me.
I will not therefore make use of
contemptuous Reflections, sly Insi-
nuations, malicious Innuendo's,
witty Sarcasms against him, because I think it both absurd and
unjust that he should do so against
me. And besides, I consider that
if my Cause be good, I shall not
need to resort to such Artifices;
and

and if it be bad, this Courſe will not mend it, but rather make my Temper appear as bad as my Cauſe.

But that which I peculiarly aim at in this place, is, (if it were poſſible) to repreſs the odious Imputation of Hereſie to one another, in Diſputations, which yet is the uſual Complement that paſſes in ſuch Caſes. I remember it was the ſaying of S. *Jerom*, *In crimine Hæreſeⱳs neminem volo eſſe patientem.* He lookt upon the Charge of Hereſie to be ſo horrid and deadly a Stab, that it would tempt the Patience of a Saint. Now if no Man can, or, (as the holy Man thought) ought to bear it ; for the ſame Reaſon, and much more, no man ought ſo liberally to beſtow it, as is commonly done. Beſides that, Hereſie in the very Notion of it implies Contumacy and Stubbornneſs added to Errour;

E   and

and if any man can find in his
heart to upbraid another with his
Errours, (which may be invo-
luntary) yet it is sure hard to
know his heart, so as to pronounce peremptorily that he is
Self-condemned, and sins against
his own Conscience. At least, I
would think it very disingenuous
for any man to judge so of me,
and therefore I ought not rashly to
pronounce so of him.

Moreover *Sixthly*, The practise
of this way of Reflection, and ta-
king an Estimate of other men by
our selves, would prevent Heart-
burnings, Jealousies, and Suspici-
ons, which are the Seed-plot of
most of the Mischiefs amongst
Mankind, and the very Bane of
Human Society : For it is but
looking inward, and I find that
I think it just that a fair and
candid Interpretation be made of
my Actions ; I conceive my self
to

The Golden Rule.

to be ill dealt with, if I be thought
to intend contrary to my Pretensi-
ons ; nay if there be any thing
dark and doubtful in the Cale, I
expect fo much Charity from men,
as that they think the beſt that
can be made of it, till the Truth
appears.

Therefore if I will be true to
my own Principles , and impartial
towards others , it is manifeſt that
after this manner I ſhould interpret
other mens Thoughts and Actions :
Not judge the Tree to be bad
when I ſee the Fruit good : Not
cenſure a man for an Hypocrite ,
meerly becauſe he looks like a
Saint ; not pronounce of mens
hearts in a direct Contrariety to
their Words and Actions. In a
word , not to ſubvert all the Foun-
dations of Friendſhip, and to Poiſon
Society by ill Surmizes.

Upon this Occasion I remember a remarkable Case between the Pagans and the Primitive Christians. It was the Custom of those good men to hold their Assemblies for Religion very privately, and for the most part by night; upon this Occasion there was a Jealousie raised amongst the Pagans, that something or other was done in those Nocturnal Meetings which would not indure the Light: and in a little while this Suspicion was improved into a common Fame, That these Christians in those Clandestine Assemblies, were wont to murder an innocent Infant, and then to eat his Flesh and drink his Blood amongst them, as the Solemn Rite of their Confederation in that Religion. Now this groundless Scandal those Primitive Christians quit themselves of, by appealing to the Common Sense of Human Nature, and this Rule

of

of Equity which we are all this while confidering ; and in their Apologies make ufe of this Dilemma : *Could you Pagans find in your hearts to perpetrate fo horrid a Villany under the pretence of Religion , as you accufe us of? If you could , you condemn your felves of Barbarifm and Cruelty beyond the rate of Mankind : But if ye could not , then you are as extreamly unjuft in fufpecting us (without Ground) of being Guilty of that which is fo abhorrent to Human Nature.*

But there is one thing more I would have confidered under this Head; namely , Whether the attending to this Rule would not prevent Sedition in the State , as well as evil Thoughts amongft private Perfons ? It is certain, all Tumults and Rebellions begin in Jealoufies of the Defigns of Governours, and thence proceed to

In

Infolencies and Contemptuous Carriage towards the Government it felf; and then when men are ingaged fo far, they ftick at nothing which may tend to the Ruin and Subverfion of that which they have both already condemned in their thoughts, and render'd themfelves obnoxious too. Now would fuch men be fo ingenuous, as in the firft place to make Allowance for fuch Human Infirmities in Magiftrates, as (confulting their own Bofoms) they muft needs acknowledge themfelves not to be exempted from; and be fo candid as to think no worfe of other mens Defigns (till the contrary appears) than they would have thought of their own: And then efpecially would they (as I have often faid) turn the Tables, and fuppofe themfelves for a while in the place of their Governours, they would then eafily conclude, That it was not ingenuous to make crofscross-grain'd and perverfe Interpretations of all dark and doubtful Paffages : Forafmuch as every man of any Senfe knows, that if he was in Publick Authority, he fhould and muft do feveral things, upon the Intereft of Government, which he ought not prefently to make every Body privy to the Reafons of, and yet he would think it unjuft to be malapertly cenfured for them. And the fame man (be he who he will) in thofe Circumftances, would not allow that every private *Caprichio* and perverfe Fancy fhould confront publick Order ; but would expect that whilft he fuftain'd that part, fome Veneration fhould be ufed towards his Perfon for the fake of the Character he bears, and that Obedience be yielded to all his (not unlawful) Injunctions. And therefore by the Rule of Equity every fuch Perfon is bound, being a private man, to carry himfelf with

E 4 the

the like regard towards those that are his Superiours. And thus (as I said) the Seeds of Sedition and Rebellion would be nipt in the Bud.

Again *Seventhly*, The due confideration of this Maxim would cure that ill-natur'd Humour of rubbing up old Sores, and upbraiding one another with former Follies and Miscarriages : A Cuſtom it is equally rife and miſchievous, and I know not whether more uncharitable or imprudent, whether more fatally obſtructing the Reformation of others, or more improvidently rebounding upon thoſe that practiſe it.

It is in the firſt place very diſ-ingenuous to reproach men, for thoſe Follies they have out-grown, and to upbraid them with thoſe Sins they have repented of and
                                for-

forsaken. It is hard that no Time nor Merit should efface Human Miscarriages! That mortal and sinful men should never forgive one another, who every day need forgiveness of God Almighty : That Men should find pleasure to rake in the Wounds of their Brethren! *And it is* that which almost invincibly tempts men to continue evil when they are brought to despair of ever being believed to be good; for what Engine hath either God or Man ever found out to mend the state of the World, other than that of Hope, the force of which is everlastingly defeated by this malicious Treatment of robbing the old Sore, and keeping it perpetually bleeding; when Sorrow shall not be allowed to cover mens shame, nor Repentance be sufficient to draw a Veil over past Follies. *And it infallibly* provokes Requital with a Vengeance ; for seeing nothing is more tender,
and

and sensible than this Point of Reputation , there is no doubt but
those who find they shall be ad-
mitted to no Propitiation , will
indeavour to extenuate their own
Guilt by rendring others as black
as themselves , and being debarred
the most natural and human way
of Satisfaction , will right themselves upon such implacable men
by way of Reprisal. *And* who is
there that hath not Spots enough,
if Envy pry into them, and whose
Blemishes will not look hideously if
Malice survey them? And who
will not seem an ugly Monster
if he be not only placed in a
bad Light , but his Picture be
drawn by ill Nature in Gall and
Soot? And who is there so destitute of these Instruments of Revenge , if Despair put him upon
doing his worst? Who is there
that hath not been mistaken in
his Youth? Who hath not been
tempted , surprized , abused one
time

time or other ? Who hath not had
his Prejudices of Education, or
been overseen in the management
of himself ? Who hath not been
over-reacht and impofed upon by
cunning men, or not confounded
by the feveral Traverfes of State
and Revolutions of the World?
So that if it muft be the way
of the World everlaftingly to bla-
zon one anothers Follies, it will
come to pafs that he that is beft
conceited of himfelf, will find he
muft fall in his value, and that
he will not pafs current at the
Rate he fets upon himfelf. But
efpecially it will happen that he,
who to oftentate his own Inno-
cency, is continually pointing at
the Failings of others, will find in
his Accounts, That he hath been
as improvident for himfelf, as he
was inexorable towards others.

But that which I am obliged to observe in this Case; and that in order to the Cure of this Distemper, is only the plain Injustice and Unequality of this way of proceeding, even upon the Principles of every man's own heart, for it is indubitable that every man would be desirous that his blind side should be concealed, that a Veil should be drawn over his Blemishes, and that an Act of Oblivion should pass, upon his former Miscarriages; and besides, he thinks it very unjust that other men should represent him by the Follies he hath outgrown, and charge him with the Opinions he hath abandoned, or upbraid him with the Actions he hath repented of: And he would be taken for what he is, and not what he was. Therefore upon the Rule of Equity, thus should it be done by every Man towards his Neighbour.

Eighthly

Eighthly and Lastly, and to conclude this Point: The study-ing of this one Aphorism (of do-ing as we would be done by) would prevent all the Frauds, Cheatings, and Oppressions that are so great an Evil to the World, and which are otherwise scarcely to be Cured or Restrained by all the Laws, Judicatories, and Pu-nishments that men can devise; for this defines them, detects, convicts, condemns, and shames them at a Bar which no man can Appeal from, or Except a-gainst. In Human Judicatories men may hope to conceal their Miscarriages, or to excuse, or to palliate, or to out-face them; ei-ther by defect of Evidence to e-scape the Trial, or by the Ad-vantage of Wit or Mony, or Pow-er or Friends, to elude the Judg-ment; some Cases the Law can-not reach, or the Witnesses can-not

not depofe and fwear home to
the Point , or the Jury cannot
penetrate into the Myftery of the
Bufinefs : But here *quid prodeft non
babere Confcium , habenti Confcien-
tiam ?* There will want no Wit-
neffes , no Inqueft , no Judge, but
a mans own felf ; and he that is
faulty , his own Heart fhall upbraid him, for debauching his own
Principles , and his Countenance
fhall fall, and his Spirit fink under
the Sentence.

No man that Confults this O-
racle will find in his heart to op-
prefs his Neighbour by Power and
Intereft , or vex him with Law-
Suits, or undermine him by Fraud,
or over-reach him by Tricks of
Wit , or make advantage of the
Weaknefs , Simplicity , Neceffity ,
or Security of his Neighbour.
No man's Table will be made a
Snare to him ; no man will flat-
ter his Friend to circumvent him ,

or

or make ufe of *Summum Jus,* and the rigour of Laws to Ruin his very Enemy; or if he do, this Court of Equity within him will reverfe the Proceedings, and feverely revenge the Contempt of its Authority. This Principle (I fay) of Self-love which fticks clofe to our Natures, and is always before our Eyes, if it be but applyed to the Cafe of other men, after the manner we have expreft, will determine us to juft and righteous, to fair and candid, and ingenuous Dealings: For whatfoever I would not that others fhould do to me, that I muft not do towards them. And fo much for that.

Fifthly, I come now in the laft place, and for a Conclufion of all, to Reprefent fome of the happy Advantages of purfuing this Rule, as fo many Motives to the careful obfervance

*vance of it. And out of ma-
ny of this kind that lie obvi-
ous to my thoughts, I will
only select these three following.*

1. Though it be true (as I have
noted before) That this Maxim is
not properly a Rule of Religion
or Devotion towards God, but
only the Measure of the Second
Table, yet it is of so great Reputation and Authority, that it
gives the Publick Stamp and Value to Piety and Devotion it self,
forasmuch as without there be a
conspicuous regard to this Rule in
our intercourse with men, the most
glorious pretences of Piety towards God, signifie nothing either
with God or Men. A mighty
Zeal in disputing and contending
about Opinions, without regard
to Equity, and Justice, and Mercy, is but a kind of Religious
Knight-Erranty, and Men encounter
only

only Windmills and Pageants, they neither Honour God, nor Profit the World, nor gain Reputation to themfelves: Nay, I think fuch Zeal will not be much undervalued, if it be refembled to *Solomon*'s doting Expeditions, when he made long Voiages for Apes and Peacocks. To be wonderfully devout in a peculiar Form or Mode of Worfhip, without Honefty and Ingenuity in our Dealings with Men, will be lookt upon as the Hypocritical acting of a Part, or at beft as being bigotted to a certain Mode without any true Notion or Senfe of Religion. In a word, To make the moft glorious Profeffion, and to efpoufe the precifeft Sect and Party, without an equal regard to this, will at leaft be lookèd upon as an effect of Pride and Singularity, and be more than fufpected as a Cloke for Knavery. For of all Religions in the

F World,

World, Chriſtianity is that of all
other which he can make the
leaſt pretence to, who *Tythes*
Mint, and Annis, and Cummin, and
Mat.23.23. *negleſts the weightier Matters of*
Faith, Juſtice, and Mercy. Our
Mat. 9. 13. Saviour himſelf hath told us, That
God *loves Mercy more than Sacri-*
fice; and is better pleaſed with
our equitable dealing with our
Neighbour, than with the moſt
coſtly Oblations to himſelf. And
Jam.1.27. his Apoſtle S. *James* declares,
That *pure Religion, and undefiled*
before God and the Father, is to
viſit the Fatherleſs and Widow in
their Affliction, &c. Nay, an Heathen, but an ingenuous Obſerver
Am. Mar-
tell. of the *Genius* of the Chriſtian Religion, gives this Account of it,
Nil niſi juſtum ſuadet & leve,
That there was nothing ſo remarkable in that Inſtitution, as the Juſtice, Mildneſs, Clemency, and E-
quity it requires of all its Proſe-
lytes.

It

It is a memorable Paſſage we have in *Tertullian*, one of the ancienteſt Writers in the Chriſtian Church, Some of the Heathens of that time upbraided the Chriſtians, That they took up their Religion to ſave Charges, and made choice not of the beſt, but the cheapeſt way of Worſhip, *For* (ſay they) *you refuſe to ſacrifice to our Gods for no other reaſon, but to ſpare the coſt of the Oblations, and the Trade and Cuſtoms of the Eaſtern Commodities of rich Gums and Spices decays, by your refraining to expend them in Incenſe to the Deity, ſo that not only Religion is leſs magnificent, but the Emperours Exchequer is damnified by your frugal way of Devotion.* To this *Tertullian* anſwers in the Name of the Chriſtians: *'Tis true, we do not evaporate ſo much of our Wealth in the vain Superſtition of Odours and Perfumes, but we ſpend*

F 2   *more*

*more in Acts of Charity towards
the Poor and Necessitous than all
your Devotion amounts to ; and this
we look upon as a more acceptable
Sacrifice, and a sweeter Odour to
the Almighty. And besides, we do
indeed spend more of those very
Commodities in the Burial and decent Treating our deceased Friends,
than you do in all your Idolatries.
And as for the Emperours Exchequer, it gains more by our Honesty and Integrity, and the Conscience we make of Defrauding it,
than by your lavish and expensive
Superstition, who thus think to
bribe your Gods, that you may be
allowed to cheat your Prince.*

Certainly there is nothing like
down-right Honesty to give Reputation to Religion, insomuch
that it is not only the most po-
pular Argument in the World to
recommend it by, but it is able
to perswade a man to the most
im-

improbable Doctrine (otherwife)
if he could be convinced that this
is the Fruit of it. But on the
other fide, when men fhall high-
ly pretend to Devotion, and yet
appear not only difingenuous and
unjuft, but unmerciful, cruel,
and fanguinary too, an indiffe-
rent man will be tempted to be
of that poor *Indians* mind, who
would not go to Heaven when he
was told that fuch a fort of men
were there.

2. The obfervation of this Rule
is fo confiderable, and fo acceptable with God, that it feems to
be the moft effectual way to ob-
tain Succefs in our Prayers and
Addreffes to him. For it is remarkable, that upon that very
Occafion this Aphorifm was delivered by our Saviour in the fore-
mentioned place, *Matth.* 7. where
when he had faid, *verfe* 7. *Ask
and it fhall be given you,* &c. and

verse 11. *If ye being evil know how to give good Gifts to your Children , how much more shall your Heavenly Father give good things to them that ask him.* He there immediately adds , *Therefore all things whatsoever ye would that men should do unto you , do ye even so unto them.* As if by those words (*men do unto you*) he had meant (according to the usual way of expression in the Hebrew Tongue) indefinitely, and had said , *Whatsoever ye would have to be done unto you , either from God or Man.* Or more at large , as if our Saviour had said , *Do ye to Men as you desire God should do to you ; for by the measures you use towards one another , ye do (upon the matter) prescribe to your selves what measure ye are to expect from him.*

To

To this purpose it is further obfervable, that in our Lord's Prayer we are taught to ufe this Argument with God Almighty, *To forgive us our Trefpaffes, for that we forgive them that Trefpafs againſt us; for* (faith our Saviour) *if ye forgive not Men their Trefpaffes, neither will your Heavenly Father forgive yours.*

Moreover, It is yet further obfervable, that in the Old Teftament, particularly *Deut.* 26. 12. God gives the People of *Ifrael* warrant to plead with him in their Addreffes, and to challenge a Bleffing from him., upon the Condition of their having dif-charged their part in Juftice, Charity, and Humanity towards their Brethren: For thus he fpeaks, *When thou haft made an end of thy Tything of the third year; and haft given it to the Stranger,*

F 4 *the*

the Fatherless, and the Widow, then thou shalt plead before the Lord, &c. Look down now from thy Habitation, and bless thy People Israel. But moft fully and exprefly is this fet out in the New Teftament, *Luke* 6. 38. where after our Saviour had fpecified feveral Inftances of Equity and Humanity, as *Love your Enemies, and do good; Give to him that asketh; Lend* (to men in neceffity) *looking for nothing again; Be merciful as your Father in Heaven is merciful*; he adds, *Judge not, and ye fhall not be judged; forgive and it fhall be forgiven you; Give and it fhall be given to you, good meafure, preffed down, and fhaken together.* He concludes all with the affurance of the fuccefs of this Courfe, *For with the fame Meafure that ye mete withal, it fhall be meafured to you again.*

But

But to conclude all, whatever
be the Succefs or Advantages of
obferving this Rule, otherwife, a
man fhall be fure to reap the
Fruit of inward Peace, and Comfort, and Satisfaction in fo doing;
nor will it be in the Power of
Chance, or the Event of Things
to difcompofe him; for whatever
may happen, or how malicious
interpretations foever may be made
of a man's Actions, yet whileft
he is fure he hath been true to
his own Confcience, and the a-
forefaid Principle, he is not only
above the Malice and Follies of
Men, but above Fear and Sufpi-
cion of Mifchief to befall him.
Or if he chance to meet with ill
Treatment from Men, he can eafily bear it, becaufe he is fure he
hath not deferved it. So that the
Retreat into a Man's felf is the
great Refuge from Troubles a-
broad, and the Reflection upon
a

a Man's Integrity in this great Point, is the principal Confolation of Human Life.

With this holy *Job* comforted himfelf in his Adverfity, *Job* 29.12. *I delivered the Poor that cryed, and the Fatherlefs, and him that had none to help him. The Blef-fing of him that was ready to pe-rifh came upon me, and I caufed the Widows heart to fing for joy. I put on Righteoufnefs and it clo-thed me, and my Judgment was as a Robe and a Diademe. I was Eyes to the blind, and Feet was I to the lame. I was a Father to the Poor, and the Caufe which I knew not I fearched out.* I brake the Jaws of the Wicked, and I pluckt the Prey out of his Teeth, &c.* In all which that good Man elegant-ly fets forth the great Support and Comfort it afforded him now in his Adverfity, that he had heretofore in his Profperity dealt
equitably

equitably, and mercifully, and con-
fider'd other Mens Cafe as his
own.

And after this rate *David* alfo
comforts himfelf in his Troubles,
Pfalm 35. 12. *They rewarded me e-
vil for good : But as for me, when
they were fick,my Clothing was Sack-
cloth; I behaved my felf as if it
had been my Friend, or my Brother* ; and then Appeals to God
hereupon. *verfe* 24. *Judge me, O
Lord, according to thy Righteoufnefs.*

On the other fide, it will be an
horrible Aggravation of our Trouble when Adverfity befalls us, if
we fhall have juft caufe to make
this Refleftion ; *Thus, and thus I
dealt with others when I was in
Profperity, and now it is come
home to me; I had no fenfe of E-
quity and Humanity towards others
then, and I muft now juftly ex-*
pect

*pect they will have as little towards
me.*

Doubtless it was no small An-
guish *Adonibesek* was under, *Judges*
1. 7. when his Guilt extorted this
sad Acknowledgment from him ,
*Threescore and ten Kings having
their Thumbs and great Toes cut
off , gather'd their Meat under my
Table; as I have done, so God hath
requited me : q. d.* In my Prosperity I was so vain and improvident , as either to forget that I
was but a Man , or that others
were so too: I neither considered
the parity of Human Nature, nor
the mutability of Human Affairs ;
I was so sottishly insolent then ,
as to treat my Equals like Dogs,
and how can I now expect they
should treat me like a Man ?
Certainly it was an heavy Aggravation of *Hamon's* Shame and
Sufferings (in the Book of *Es-
ther*) that he must be hanged on
the

the same Gallows he had provided for the pious, but brow-beaten *Mordecai*. And *Perillus* roared moſt hideouſly when he was roaſted in the brazen Bull which he had deviſed for the Torture of others. And to add no more Examples of this kind, we may eaſily bethink our ſelves what a dreadful Remorſe and Horrible Agony of Mind *Joſeph's* Brethren were in, *Geneſ.* 42. 21. when they themſelves came to be in ſtraits, and reflect upon their former unnatural dealing with their Brother, they cry out one to another, *We are verily Guilty concerning our Brother, in that we ſaw the anguiſh of his Soul, when he beſought us and we would not hear, therefore is this diſtreſs come upon us.* It is therefore all the Wiſdom and Reaſon in the World, ſince we know not how ſoon it may be our turn to be at the lower part of the Wheel, to

temper

temper our selves with Equity and Moderation whilest we are uppermost, according to the Counsel of our Saviour, *To make us Friends of the Mammon of Unrighteousness*; and then to *do to others as at another time we would wish and think fit they should do by us*; which was the Point I began with, and with which I now make an end.

F I N I S.

Books Printed for Robert Clavell *at the* Peacock *in* S.Pauls Church-yard.

A Difcourfe concerning a Judge of Controverfies in Matters of Religion; being an Anfwer to fome Papers afferting the Neceffity of fuch a Judge. With an Addrefs to Wavering Proteftants; fhewing what little Reafon they have to think of any Change of their Religion. Written for the private Satisfaction of fome fcrupulous Perfons, and now publifhed for common ufe. With a Preface concerning the Nature of Certainty and Infallibility. *By an eminent Author.*

The Plaufible Arguments of a *Romifh Prieft* from Scripture, Anfwered by an *Englifh Proteftant.* Seafonable and Ufeful for all *Proteftant* Families.

A Difcourfe of Duels; fhewing the Sinful Nature and Mifchievous Effects of them: And Anfwering the

the ufual Excufes made for them
by Challengers, Accepters, and
Seconds.   By *T. Comber* D. D.
The *Catholic Balance*; or a Difcourfe
determining the Controverfies
concerning, 1. The Catholic Doctrine. 2.The Primacy of S.*Peter*,
and the Bifhop of *Rome*.   3. The
Subjection and Authority of the
Church in a   Chriftian State:
According to the Suffrages of
the primeft Antiquity.   Written
with moft impartial fincerity at
the requeft of a private Gentleman.
Frequent and Fervent Prayer according to Scripture and Primitive
Ufage, as it is now practifed by
the pious Members of the Church
of *England*. In Octavo. Price 4 *d.*
By *Thomas Comber* D.D.
A few Plain Reafons why a Proteftant of the Church of *England*
fhould not turn Roman Catholic.
By a real Catholic of the Church
of *England*.

www.ingramcontent.com/pod-product-compliance
Lightning Source LLC
Chambersburg PA
CBHW032247080426
42735CB00008B/1041